BLACK FACTS:

The Black History Newsletter

**People and events in black history
presented in an exciting, daily newsletter format!**

Designed for use during
Black History Month:
FEBRUARY, 2012

Written by S. K. Cuthbertson
ISBN -13 978-146-7913829
ISBN – 10 146-7913820

Introduction

Black Facts **African American History Newsletters** are designed to present black history to students in grades 6-12 in a dynamic and easy-to-use format. The information contained is great for use in class discussions, or as a catalyst for student research into the historical events and individual lives discussed herein. They can also serve as excellent supplemental reading material in various curriculum areas. **This edition is specifically designed to correspond to the school day calendar for February, 2012: Black History Month.** The newsletters are intended to be a fun, exciting way to inform readers about African American contributions to science, sports, the arts, academia, politics, religion, medicine, social movements, and the military. From the Sixteenth to the Twenty-First Century, black people have made an indelible mark on American history. These newsletters give students a small but impactful glimpse at 500 years of the influence and achievements of blacks in America.

BLACK FACTS

Dr. Carter G. Woodson

HISTORY

Negro History Week ▪ In 1915, author and historian **Dr. Carter G. Woodson** and several friends established the Association for the Study of Negro Life and History. In 1926, Dr. Woodson founded Negro History Week. He wanted black Americans to be proud of their history, and other Americans to know and appreciate blacks' contribution to the nation.

The month of February was chosen to honor Frederick Douglass and Abraham Lincoln, both of whom were born this month. Dr. Woodson's outstanding historical research influenced others to carry on his work. The original period of one week was later expanded to the entire month.

FIRSTS

South Carolina, 1526 ▪ The first group of blacks set foot in what is now the United States of America. They were brought here by the Spanish as slaves, to set up a settlement in the New World. However, the blacks soon fled, and after their escape, they lived with Native Americans.

Baltimore, 1754 ▪ **Benjamin Banneker,** a 22 year-old free black, was the first person in the North American Colonies to build a working clock. He had no instructions; just a pocket watch lent to him to use as a guide. The clock kept accurate time for over 20 years. Banneker, an inventor and mathematician, also produced an almanac in 1791; the first scientific book written by an African American.

BLACK INVENTORS

Rotary Engine	A.J. Beard, 1892
Railway Signal	A.B. Blackburn, 1888
Ironing Board	Sarah Boone, 1892
Lawn Mower	J.A. Burr, 1899
Electric Elevator	A. Miles, 1887

DO YOU KNOW???

1. What is the name of the document signed by Abraham Lincoln, which freed the slaves in the Confederate States?

2. Who founded the Black Panther Party?

3. Who was the athlete snubbed by Chancellor of Germany Adolph Hitler in 1936, after winning four Olympic gold medals in track and field?

THE ANSWERS WILL BE GIVEN TOMORROW.

 SKC Publications, 2012©

BLACK FACTS

Harriet Tubman

HISTORY

March 5, 1770, Boston, Mass.▪ **Crispus Attucks**, a former slave, was shot and killed during the Boston Massacre. He is widely believed to be the very first American to die in the American Revolutionary War.

August, 1831, Virginia - **Nat Turner** led the biggest slave revolt in American history. During a two-month period, over 60 whites were killed, and the entire South was thrown into a state of panic. Turner was captured on October 30th, and hanged 12 days later.

Maryland, 1849 - **Harriet Tubman** escaped from slavery. She became a "Conductor" on the *Underground Railroad*: an established, secret escape route from the South to northern states and Canada. Tubman helped over 300 slaves reach freedom in the 19 trips she made back into the deep South, to help others escape.

Yesterday's Trivia Answers

1. The Emancipation Proclamation

2. Bobby Seale and Huey Newton

3. Jessie Owens

FIRSTS

July 10, 1893, Chicago, Illinois - **Dr. Daniel Hale Williams** performed the first successful open heart surgery. He was also the founder of Provident Hospital, where the surgery was performed.

1941, Washington, DC ▪ **Dr. Charles Drew** was appointed director of the first American Red Cross blood bank, in charge of blood for use by the U.S. Army and Navy. He later served as a professor of medicine at Howard University, and as a surgeon at Freedman's Hospital from 1942 to 1950.

The rice plant and its cultivation were first introduced to North America by West Africans. Blacks showed the English how to plant, care for and harvest rice. Rice became so important to South Carolina's economy, that it remained its major crop until well into the 19th century.

BLACK INVENTORS

Horseshoe   Oscar Brown, 1892

Fountain Pen   William Purvis, 1890

Gas Burner   Benjamin Jackson, 1899

Automatic Traffic Signal   Garrett Morgan, 1923

Telephone Answering Machine B. Thorton, 1935

DO YOU KNOW???

1. Who was the first African American to be honored on a United States postage stamp?

2. What African-American controlled company was the first to sell shares on the New York Stock Exchange?

3. Who was the first African American to win an Emmy for Best Lead Actor in a drama series?

ANSWERS GIVEN TOMORROW

February 3, 2012

Black Facts

Booker T. Washington

HISTORY

Tuskegee, AL, 1881 - **Booker T. Washington** opened the Tuskegee Normal and Industrial Institute, which is now Tuskegee University. The school began with one small shanty, 30 students and one teacher (Washington). Its purpose was to train teachers, the first school of this kind in the United States. Tuskegee is now a 5000 acre campus with over 150 buildings. The college was declared a national historical landmark in 1965.

NAACP ▪ The National Association for the Advancement of Colored People was founded in New York, NY, 1909. Black charter members included **W.E.B. DuBois**, **Ida B. Wells**, and famous whites such as Jane Addams and John Dewey.

Matthew Henson placed the American flag at the North Pole in 1909. He was the first person to set foot there. Henson routinely traveled on dangerous expeditions with Robert Peary, the famous explorer. Henson was a "trail breaker," who would arrive at a site before others, and set up camp. Henson was buried at Arlington National Cemetery in Washington, D.C., with full military honors.

FIRSTS

Louisiana, 1890 - Thomy Lafon, a real estate speculator and money lender, was probably the first black millionaire in the United States.

Ithaca, NY, 1906 - Alpha Phi Alpha, the first black fraternity, was founded at Cornell University.

Washington, DC, 1908 - The first black sorority, Alpha Kappa Alpha, was founded at Howard University.

INVENTIONS

Ice Cream ▪ Augustus Jackson, PA, 1832

Dry Cleaning ▪ Thomas Jennings, 1821

Sugar Refiner ▪ Norbert Rillieux, 1850

Hair Care / Cosmetics for blacks ▪ Madame C.J. Walker, circa 1890's

Peanut Butter, other peanut products ▪ George Washington Carver, circa 1900.

DO YOU KNOW????

1. Who was the first African American player to join the National Baseball league?

2. What African American has won more Emmy Awards than any other television personality?

3. What major American city was founded by African American Jean Baptiste Pointe du Sable in 1790?

Answers From Yesterday

1. Booker T. Washington, in 1940.
2. Black Entertainment Television (BET)
3. Bill Cosby for "I, Spy" in 1966.

   SKC Publications, 2012 ©

Black Facts

HISTORY

New York, 1776 ▪ A black woman saved George Washington's life. **Phoebe Fraunces** was romantically involved with Thomas Hickey, secretly a British agent working as Washington's bodyguard. Phoebe worked in her father's tavern, where Washington frequently dined. After winning Phoebe's heart, Hickey gave her a bowl of poisoned peas to serve to the general. Despite her love for Hickey, Phoebe warned Washington who threw the peas into the yard. Some chickens in the yard ate the peas and died immediately. Hickey was hanged before a crowd of 20,000 in New York City. Had Washington, who was the heart of the American Revolution died then, the America we know might never have been established.

Lynn, Mass., 1883 - After years of work, black inventor **Jan Matzeliger** built a machine that manufactured an entire shoe. Before this, shoes had to be completed by hand, which made the work very slow, and shoes very expensive. The majority of people went around barefoot most of the time, and saved their precious shoes for special occasions, if they had a pair. This invention was so successful, it revolutionized the shoe industry. For the first time, the average person could afford to have shoes for daily wear.

Answers From Friday

1. Jackie Robinson
2. Oprah Winfrey
3. Chicago, Illinois

Central Florida ▪ The town of Eatonville, located about 10 miles northeast of downtown Orlando, was incorporated in 1888. It is considered to be the oldest African American municipality in the United States. Eatonville is also the hometown of **Zora Neale Hurston**, the celebrated African American author.

FIRSTS

1908, Sydney, Australia ▪ **Jack Johnson** defeated Tommy Burns and became the first African American heavyweight champion of the world. He defended the title for 8 years, including a winning bout with former champion Jim Jeffries, who was called, "The Great White Hope." A play, and later a motion picture with this title, was made about Johnson's life.

September 9, 1972 - "Fat Albert and the Cosby Kids," the first Saturday morning cartoon show with black characters, aired on NBC. In 1969, a single show in prime time was successful enough to make the series possible 3 years later. The show was based on **Bill Cosby**'s stories of his childhood in Philadelphia. Each episode featured a positive character lesson for the millions of kids that watched. The original show ran until 1977.

DO YOU KNOW ?????

1. What NBA star was so unstoppable as a rebounder, that the dimensions of the court were changed because of him, *and* he was the first black coach of a major league sports team in the U.S.?

2. Who is the author of the widely acclaimed novel, *Roots*?

3. Who was the first African American to win the title of Miss America?

Seaman Dorrie Miller

BLACK FACTS

HISTORY

Washington, DC, 1939: Marian Anderson sang on the steps of the Lincoln Memorial for an Easter  Sunday concert. Anderson had been barred from performing at Constitution Hall because of her race. Public reaction was immediate and intense. First Lady Eleanor Roosevelt arranged for this concert to take place in protest. Over 70,000 people turned out that day to hear Anderson's great voice.

December 7, 1941 – Dorie Miller, a crewman aboard the *USS Arizona*, shot down four enemy planes during the bombing of Pearl Harbor by the Empire of Japan. He was awarded the Navy Cross for, "Distinguished devotion to duty, extreme courage, and disregard for his personal safety during attack." In 1973, the *USS Miller* was christened, making Dorie Miller the first African American enlisted man to have a navy ship named after him.

 **Oslo, Norway, 1950** – Dr. Ralph J. Bunche became the first African American to win the Nobel Peace Prize. Dr. Bunche's outstanding diplomatic career placed him among the most significant Americans in public service in the 20th century.

Answers From Yesterday's Trivia:

1. Bill Russell
2. Alex Haley wrote *Roots* based on his own family tree.
3. Vanessa Williams

FIRSTS

April 15, 1950 – **Charles Cooper** signs with the Boston Celtics to become the first African American to play for an NBA team.

 **Hollywood, CA, 1963**: Mr. Sidney Poitier became the first African American to win an Academy Award (Oscar) for best actor in a leading role in the film, *Lilies of the Field.*

New York, 1968 - Representative Shirley Chisom became the first black woman elected to the U.S. Congress. In 1972, Chisom sought the Democratic nomination for the presidency, making her the first woman in American politics ever to do so.

INVENTIONS

Electric Railway Trolley	E. R .Robinson, 1893
Permanent Hair Wave	M. Joyner, 1928
Gas Mask	Garrett Morgan, 1914
Hand-powered Mixer	Willis Johnson, 1884
Stair climbing Wheelchair	Rufus Weaver, 1968

Do you know ????

1. What percent of the United States Population is African American?

2. What is the disease for which one African American out of every 12 carries the genetic trait?

3. Who is the famous black musician and singer born as Steveland Morris Judkins, on May 13, 1950?

Answers given tomorrow…

.

February 8, 2012

BLACK

Flag of Liberia

FACTS

HISTORY

1820, West Coast of Africa – The "Mayflower of Liberia" sailed from New York City with 86 blacks, on their way to Africa. The first ex-slaves arrived at the sight of the future nation's capital, Monrovia. Under President James Monroe, funding was provided and land acquired to form the Commonwealth of Liberia, later to become the Republic of Liberia, an independent nation for freed slaves. In 1847, Liberia became Africa's first independent republic.

The slave ship *Amistad* was brought in 1839 into Montauk, NY by a group of Africans who had revolted and taken over the ship. Their young leader, **Joseph Cinque** and his followers were defended before the U.S. Supreme Court by former President John Quincy Adams They were given their freedom and returned to Africa.

By unanimous vote, the U.S. Supreme Court

decided that "separate but equal" educational facilities are "inherently unequal." The case was Brown vs. Board of Education, Topeka, Kansas, May 17, 1954. The legal team that won the case was the NAACP's group of lawyers, led by **Thurgood Marshall**, future Supreme Court Justice.

FIRSTS

1962 – Jackie Robinson became the first African American to be inducted into the Baseball Hall of Fame.

The Nobel Prize for literature was awarded to Toni Morrison on November 7, 1993, in Oslo, Norway. She was the first African American woman to win this international honor.

The nation's only known African American sextuplets were born to Jacqueline and Linden Thompson – 4 boys and 2 girls (1 stillborn) in Washington, DC, 1997.

BLACK INVENTIONS

Spark Plug – Edmund Berger, 1839

Automatic Gear Shift – Richard Spikes, 1932

Street Sweeper – C. B. Scott, 1896

Envelope Seal – F.W. Leslie, 1891

Bicycle Frame – I. R. Johnson, 1899

Do You Know???

1. What constitutional amendment guarantees African Americans the right to vote?

2. What is the largest predominately African American college in the U.S.?

3. What song is considered the Black National Anthem?

Answers from Yesterday

1. 12.3 percent, or approximately 40 million.
2. Sickle Cell Anemia
3. Stevie Wonder

BLACK FACTS

HISTORY

Richmond Virginia, 1856 ● Perhaps the most imaginative way to escape slavery was pulled off by **Henry "box" Brown**, who mailed himself to freedom. Brown ordered a box and put in a jug of water, a few biscuits and a bar to open the box from the inside. He had a friend address the box to Philadelphia and write, "Handle with care," and "This side up." After traveling 26 hours upside down, the strange cargo arrived at its destination. Some abolitionists, warned that the box was on the way, picked it up at the railway station. When the lid of the box was pried off, Brown is said to have exclaimed, "How do you do, my gentlemen?"

"Father Divine." ● One of the most extensive religious cults in America was founded by **George Baker** in Long Island, in 1932. Referring to himself as God, Baker founded an interracial commune, which was not well-received in Long Island. He was arrested, and after Justice Lewis J. Smith sentenced him to a year in jail, the judge died. Divine's followers declared, "The judge sentenced God to jail, and God sentenced the judge to hell!" From his jail cell Divine remarked, "I hated to do it." Divine's movement actually accomplished a great deal of good during the Depression: running soup kitchens for the poor, a homeless shelter, an employment agency to help the unemployed and several schools for adults and children. At its strongest point, Baker and his Peace Missions had approximately 100,000 members.

Answers From Yesterday...

1. The 15th Amendment
2. Howard University in Washington, DC
3. "Lift Every Voice and Sing

FIRSTS

France, 1920 ● **Bessie Coleman** became the first African American, and the first woman, to become a licensed pilot. She was the first African American woman to fly a plane, the first American to earn an international aviator's license and the first black female stunt pilot.

PIONEER D.J. ● New York, NY, 1974 – **Joseph Sadler**, who used the stage name of **Grandmaster Flash**, created a whole new way of performing as a disc jockey. He originated the technique of "scratching": moving a record back and forth under a needle as a sound effect. He was also the first to hook up two turntables to the same speakers and by playing two different records, mix musical elements from both to make a third original composition. Sadler also assembled a group of rappers which he called the "Furious Five." In 2007, Grandmaster Flash and the Furious Five was the first rap group inducted into the Rock and Roll Hall of Fame.

BLACK INVENTIONS

Bread Crumbling Machine - John Lee, 1895
Adding Machine - Shelby Davison, 1893
Automobile Convertible Top- J. Jones, 1919
Portable X-Ray Machine – F. M. Jones, 1930

DO YOU KNOW????

1. What African American broke Babe Ruth's record in 1974 when he hit home run number 715?

2. What legendary music company started in a wooden frame house in Detroit, marked with a sign that read, "Hitsville, USA"?

3. What famous athlete changed his name from Lew Alcindor to his current moniker?

Answers tomorrow…

SKC Publications, 2012©

BLACK FACTS

Mr. Chuck Berry

HISTORY

Levi Coffin

Whites and the Underground Railroad • Some of the most effective conductors on the Underground Railroad were white. **Levi Coffin**, a Quaker, helped close to two thousand runaway slaves find freedom. He often hid runaways in a secret compartment built into his house. Not only did many whites risk their lives to help escaping slaves, but white participation in the anti - slavery movement gave it increased credibility in the eyes of the larger American society.

Blacks Drop "African" as an Identifier • In the late 1800's, black leaders began to drop the word "African" from their organization names. They feared that those who were actively working to re-colonize ex-slaves back to Africa, would take the use of this word to mean that most blacks desired to be shipped to Africa. The opposite was true; the great majority of blacks considered themselves American, and wanted to be treated as full citizens, not sent to another continent they had never seen. Only in the last few decades have black Americans begun to re-embrace "African" as part of their identity.

FIRSTS

50's • Despite all the tributes given to Elvis Presley, **Chuck Berry** was the first real pioneer of Rock and Roll. He had many hit records in his career including, "Roll Over Beethoven" and "Johnny B. Goode." He was inducted into the Rock and Roll Hall of Fame in 1986, the first year the honor was given.

Medical Breakthrough • **Dr. Ben Carson**, the celebrated neurosurgeon, performed the first successful separation of Siamese twins joined at the head. Dr. Carson led a medical team of seventy doctors, nurses and technicians in the 22-hour, landmark surgery on the infants to separate their brains. Dr. Carson was raised in the slums of Detroit and at one time was a failing student who was constantly in trouble. At 14, he almost killed another boy in a knife fight. His mother started him on n at-home book reading program and limited his television viewing until his grades improved. By the end of high school, his grades earned him a full scholarship at Yale University.

DO YOU KNOW???

1. What African American recording artist is credited as the first to develop the music video format, now an essential part of the music industry?

2. Who was the first African American to serve as Chairman of the Joint Chiefs of Staff, second only to the president as commander of our military?

3. The motion picture, *"The Ghosts of Mississippi"* was about the 30-year fight to convict the murderer of what famous civil rights leader?

Answers on Monday…

Answers From Yesterday

1. Henry Aaron

2. Motown Records

3. Kareem Abdul-Jabbar

BLACK

FACTS

HISTORY

The Golden Thirteen • Under political pressure, the U.S. Navy accepted the first class of black men in officer's training school during WW II. Sixteen young men, who had proven themselves as excellent seamen, were accepted in 1944. The class had a scholastic average of 3.89— still a Navy record! Although all 16 passed, 13 were actually commissioned as Ensigns in the Navy. They became known as the "Golden Thirteen," and opened the door for all future black officers following in their footsteps.

Black Power • African Americans **Tommie Smith** and **John Carlos** shocked the country when they used their victory in the 1968 Summer Olympics to demonstrate for civil rights. Smith (gold medal) and Carlos (bronze), heads lowered and eyes closed, raised their fists over their heads during the national anthem at the award ceremony. This became known as the "Black Power" Salute. Their medals for the 200 Meter Dash were taken away by the Olympic Committee because they used their wins to make a political statement.

FIGURES

States with the highest black populations:

District of Columbia*	57.2%
Mississippi	35.6%
Louisiana	31.6%
South Carolina	28.3%
Georgia	27.2%
Maryland	26.7%
Alabama	25.4%
North Carolina	20.4%
	* not a state

States with the lowest black populations:

New Hampshire	0.89%
South Dakota	0.80%
Utah	0.77%
Wyoming	0.66%
North Dakota	0.64%
Maine	0.63%
Vermont	0.57%
Idaho	0.43%

DO YOU KNOW???

1. What U.S. President signed the bill making Martin Luther King Jr.'s birthday a national holiday?

2. What African American performer known as the "Godfather of Soul," recorded the hit, "Say it loud, I'm black and I'm proud"?

3. What popular black magazine has been in publication since 1945 and currently has a circulation of about one million readers?

Answers From Friday

1. Michael Jackson
2. Colin Powell
3. Medgar Evers

BILL PICKETT

Black Facts

HISTORY

Black Cowboy ▪ In 1870, **Bill Pickett** was born in Texas to former slaves. After the 5th grade, he got a job as a ranch hand, where he developed his riding and roping skills. He was one of the best. He invented the sport of "bulldogging": roping and wrestling steers to the ground. Although he was only 5'7" tall and 145 lbs., he took on even the fiercest animal. He would actually sink his teeth into its nose or lower lip to make it docile and beatable. Pickett was a star performer in western shows held in several countries. In 1932, he was kicked in the head by a stallion, and died 11 days later. In 1971, Bill Pickett was the first African American cowboy admitted to the National Rodeo Hall of Fame, in Oklahoma City.

Criminal Gangs ▪ An unfortunate contribution to America has been the notorious national gang alliances that were started by blacks in Chicago, Ill. In the 1960's, Jeff Fort organized the Black P-Stone Nation, which grew into a well-organized criminal enterprise. Fort eventually went to federal prison for life. During the same decade, **David Barksdale** and **Larry Hoover** merged their gangs to form the Black Gangster Disciple Nation. Barksdale and Hoover also ended up in prison for life. These two "nations" have evolved into huge crime syndicates that have negatively affected society. These gangs have spread across the country, branching off and growing into new gangs and infiltrating every low-income area of our society, including prisons, which are often a breeding ground for criminal associations.

FIRSTS

A Shot in the Arm ▪ Africans first introduced inoculation in America as a cure for smallpox. **Onesimus**, a Boston slave, taught Cotton Mather, the famous minister, the technique. In 1721, Mather injected some fluid from an infected person into the blood of someone else. Later, that person was exposed to the disease and found to be immune.

First Guitar - The Banjo, known as the "Banjar," was an African contribution to American music. Thomas Jefferson commented on this interesting, 4-string instrument. He stated in his writings that it  was, "brought hither from Africa," by slaves, and was the "original [form] of the guitar."

 **Frederick Ira Aldridge**, born in New York City and educated at The African Free School, made his debut in London in 1826, playing the role of Othello. He was later acclaimed as one of the great actors of the 19th Century.

DO YOU KNOW ????

1. Who was the first black pro football Player to be named the MVP of the NFL?

2. What was the most successful R&B singing group during the 1960's, with 9 number-one hit records from 1964 to 1967?

3. What famous group of black military Pilots was so effective, their success led directly to the desegregation of the U.S. Armed forces?

Answers tomorrow…

From Yesterday's Questions
1. Ronald Reagan
2. James Brown
3. Ebony Magazine

BLACK FACTS

HISTORY

Buffalo Soldiers • In 1866, Congress created all-black cavalry and infantry units in the US Army. They were called Buffalo Soldiers, a name the Indians gave them. Cheyenne warriors said their dark skin and thick hair resembled the buffalo. The regiments fought in most of the battles against hostile tribes, and won many honors, including several for individual heroism. In addition to combat, these men explored and mapped vast areas of the Southwest, and strung hundreds of miles of telegraph lines. They built and repaired frontier outposts, which often grew into towns and cities. They also protected the crews working on the railroad, who would have been at the mercy of outlaws and hostile Indians. Despite the hardness of this life, they had the lowest desertion rate of the frontier army. The last units were disbanded in 1944, which ended the long, proud history of the Buffalo Soldiers.

The Harlem Globetrotters was not the first black professional basketball team, but it is by far the best known. The Globetrotters was formed in 1926, and for years the team was the place for the most talented black players of the game. Blacks were barred from playing on white teams, so the Globetrotters and other black professional teams made a living playing black college teams. When basketball became integrated in the 1960's, the best players left the black teams to play for the NBA. The Globetrotters then switched to entertainment, featuring comic routines and fancy ball handling. The team remains popular and internationally famous today.

George Washington Carver was born into slavery in 1861. Carver received a bachelor's degree and a master of agricultural science degree by 1896. He traveled to Alabama to direct the new agriculture department at Tuskegee Normal and Industrial Institute, built by Booker T. Washington. At the time, agriculture in the South was in serious trouble because the constant cultivation of cotton had left the soil seemingly unable to sustain any plant growth. Carver discovered that this soil could easily grow peanuts, soybeans, and sweet potatoes. He then created the commercial possibilities of these crops through his ingenious work in the laboratory. Eventually, Carver invented over 400 usable products, keeping the southern United States from economic ruin.

FIRSTS

1975 ▪ **General Daniel "Chappie" James** was promoted in the U. S. Air Force to become the first African American four - star general in American history. On the same day, he was named Commander-in-Chief of the North American Air Defense Command.

DO YOU KNOW ? ? ?

1. What is the title of the famous whistled theme song of the Harlem Globetrotters?

2. Who was the first African American woman to win four gold medals in a single Olympics?

3. What African American rap group was the first to win a Grammy Award?

Answers tomorrow…

Answers From Yesterday

1. Jim Brown in 1963
2. The Supremes
3. The Tuskegee Airmen

BLACK FACTS

Sojourner Truth

HISTORY

SOJOURNER TRUTH ▪ Born in New York in 1797, **Isabel** was a slave sold many times before she finally escaped. When her last master broke his promise to set her free, God, with whom she frequently spoke, advised her that she should leave. She then changed her name to Sojourner Truth, and began her career as one of the most popular and well-known speakers against slavery, and for women's rights. She was so witty and convincing that once a group of men in Indiana said that they doubted she really was a woman. She embarrassed her critics by baring her breasts in public, which silenced them. Her eloquence demonstrated the intelligence of African Americans, in general, and of black women in particular.

BLIND TOM ▪ Born in 1849 near Columbus GA, **Thomas Green** was sold, along with his mother, to the Bethune Family while still a baby. When Tom was four, the family bought a piano. Tom heard Mrs. Bethune teaching her daughters to play for three years. One day at the age of seven, Tom made his way to the piano and played perfectly the tunes he had heard the day before. Recognizing his genius, the Bethune family began hiring him out for activities that required music. Gifted with a great memory, Tom developed a huge repertory. His ability to play a piece after only hearing it once, lead historians to believe he was autistic, an "idiot savant." Tom played Bach, Beethoven, and Chopin; as well as the popular tunes of the day. After slavery ended, he remained with the Bethune family, making

them wealthy. Many reformers protested, calling for the family to release him. But Tom himself objected, saying that freedom for a blind man with nowhere to go, would not make his life any better. Tom's performances were in demand all over the country and he toured the United States and Europe. He retired in 1898, some ten years before his death.

FIRSTS

WINNER ▪ **Wendell Scott** was the first African American auto racing champion. In 1963, he won the NASCAR race at Speedway Park in Jacksonville, FL. Scott had to overcome a lot of prejudice to achieve success. His story was told in the motion picture, *Greased Lightning,* staring Richard Pryor as Scott. In 1999, Wendell Scott was inducted into the International Motorsports Hall of Fame, the first black race car driver so honored.

DO YOU KNOW ????

1. Who holds the record for the most gold singles in R&B music, 21 in all?

2. What mini-series, based on the novel by Alex Haley, received the highest ratings in television history?

3. What religion teaches that deceased Ethiopian **Emperor Haile Selassie** is a supreme being?

     Answers tomorrow…

Answers From Yesterday

1. *Sweet Georgia Brown*

2. Florence Griffith Joiner in 1988

3. Jazzy Jeff & the Fresh Prince in 1988 for *Parents Just Don't Understand.*

February 17, 2012

BLACK FACTS

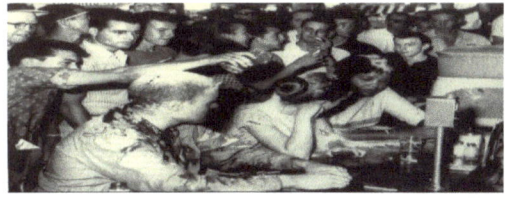

Woolworth's lunch counter in Greensboro, NC, 1960

HISTORY

SIT - INS • The Sit-in Movement began on February 1, 1960, when four African American college students sat down at the Woolworth's lunch counter in Greensboro, NC. The goal of the sit-in was to force Woolworth's to serve African Americans at the only lunch counter in the store, where they were not allowed to sit

Every day the students would sit at the counter, waiting to be served. Insults were screamed at them; they were pelted with objects, had hot coffee and other foods dumped on them and were burned with cigarette butts. The students knew however that if they had given up, or retaliated, nothing would ever change.

As news of what was happening reached the world, sit-ins began in cities across the South, by black and white people determined to make things change. On July 25, at 2.00 p.m., without any prior notice, the students in Greensboro were served. By August 1st, lunch counters in fifteen American cities were desegregated.

FREEDOM RIDERS

On May 4, 1961, thirteen black and whites trained in non-violent resistance, left Washington DC on a bus trip through the South to end segregation on buses and bus facilities. The riders challenged segregated seating in buses and terminals, as well as segregated bathrooms and dining areas.

Riders were attacked and beaten savagely in Birmingham and Montgomery, Alabama. In Anniston, AL, not only were the riders beaten, a bus was bombed. In Mississippi, riders were arrested but after bonding out, they continued the ride. The rides soon drew national attention. On the order of Attorney General Robert Kennedy, the Interstate Commerce Commission ended segregation on all travel facilities in the South.

FIRSTS

J.C. Watts, Jr. was the first African American in the Republican Party elected to congressional leadership in modern times. In 1997, Watts became the first African American to give the response to a president's State of the Union Address, when he followed President Clinton's speech before the nation.

Phillis Wheatley was born in Africa in 1753, and sold into slavery at age seven or eight. During her life, it was not at all common for slaves to be educated. However, her owners taught her to read and write, and encouraged her as a poet. Phillis was the first African American to publish a book; and she was the first black woman to earn a living from her writing. Her success as a poet both in the United States and England eventually led to her release from slavery in 1773.

DO YOU KNOW ???

1. What is the West Indian practice of creating charms, potions, conjuring and predicting the future called?

2. What African American is the youngest person ever to receive an Academy Award (Oscar) nomination for best director?

3. What famous athlete was named Cassius Clay at birth?

Answers on Monday...

Answers From Yesterday

1. Janet Jackson
2. *Roots,* 1977
3. Rastafarianism

BLACK FACTS

HISTORY

AFRICANS DISCOVER AMERICA ▪ There is firm evidence which shows that Africans explored the Americas before Christopher Columbus. In 1513, Spanish explorer Vasco de Balboa found a community of black people already living in South America. Also, Columbian pottery has been found which bear faces with distinct African features. Africans most likely reached South America by sailing on strong ocean currents from the coast of West Africa. When Columbus arrived in the Caribbean, he found dark-skinned people who regularly traded with the Indians; he was told they had come across the ocean from the southeast. In his diaries, Columbus implied these people had come from the coast of Guinea, now known as West Africa.

MARCII ON WASIIINGTON • On August

28, 1963, the largest demonstration in the history of the U.S. to that date took place in Washington, DC. The event united many different civil rights, religious, and labor organizations with varying views, but they came together to make a statement to America. While some of the speakers made statements very critical of the country, **Dr. Martin Luther King, Jr.** captured the mood of optimism and hope on that day with his now famous, "I Have a Dream" speech. The march was expected to engage around 100,000 participants, and leaders were surprised when the number swelled to over a quarter of a million people.

FIRSTS

Thurgood Marshall was the first African American United States Supreme Court Justice. Born in Baltimore, MD in 1908, his goal was to be a dentist. After college however, he changed his mind and went to law school instead. He graduated from Howard at the top of his class and in 1936, he began a private practice and worked part time as an assistant counsel with the NAACP. He worked on very important cases involving the constitutional rights of black Americans. In 1954 , he was the lead attorney on the Supreme Court case, Brown vs. the Board of Education. Of the 32 cases he argued before the Supreme Court, he won 29. In 1967, President Lyndon B. Johnson nominated him for the Supreme Court After his appointment, he didn't forget his ideals, but continued his work for racial justice. He retired from the court because of poor health in 1991, and died in 1993.

Gwendolyn Brooks was the first African American to receive a Pulitzer Prize for Poetry. She also received numcrous other national honors for her work, and was appointed the Poet Laureate of the state of Illinois in 1968.

DO YOU KNOW????

1. What Black athlete holds the NBA record for playing the most consecutive games at 978?

2. Who was the first African American model on *Sports Illustrated's* swimsuit issue?

3. What African American's image was the first to be engraved on an American coin?

Answers tomorrow…

Answers From Friday

1. Voodoo
2. Boyz N the Hood, directed (and written) by John Singleton.
3. Muhammad Ali

Mr. Nat "King" Cole

BLACK FACTS

HISTORY

PANTHERS • In 1966, the Black Panther Party was founded by **Bobby Seal** and **Huey Newton** in Oakland, California. The Party promoted military self-defense against police brutality. They also demanded full employment for all blacks and the release of all black inmates (which were all political prisoners to the Panthers).

They also wanted the payment of 40 acres and a mule, which had been promised to all former slaves during the Reconstruction Era. The Panthers also wanted separate representation in the United Nations for black Americans. The Party blended the philosophies of Malcolm X and Karl Marx. The Panthers were known for wearing black leather jackets and black berets.

They gained the attention of the FBI when an armed group of Panthers marched to the capitol building in Sacramento to protest a bill proposed to limit their right to carry arms in public. At its height in 1972, the Party had about 3000 members, but the shaky organization quickly fell apart because of internal divisions and legal problems.

Bobby Seale went to prison on charges that he worked to incite a riot at the Democratic National Convention in 968. Huey Newton went to Cuba in 1974 to avoid murder charges. In 1989, he was killed in a drug-related shooting.

FIRSTS

TV PIONEER ▪ **Nat "King" Cole** was the first African American to star in his own television show. The show aired from 1956–'57. It featured Cole performing, as well as other musical guests. Although the quality of the show was high, it was impossible to find enough advertising sponsors in this time of prevailing racism, so the program was canceled after one season. His career continued to prosper however, until his death from lung cancer in 1965.

Leroy "Satchel" Paige was the most famous African American Baseball player, long before Jackie Robinson broke the color line in "organized" baseball. Paige began playing professionally in the 1920's and was the dominant pitcher in the Negro Baseball League for 20 years. In 1948, although well past his prime, Paige played for the Cleveland Indians in the 1948 World Series. He also played for the St. Louis Browns from 1951-'53. In 1965, to qualify him for a major league penslon, Kansas City signed him for one game, in which he pitched three innings. He was 59 years old at the time. Satchel Paige was inducted into the Baseball Hall of Fame in 1971.

DO YOU KNOW ????

1. Who assassinated Martin Luther King? Where did it happen?

2. What music company executive is responsible for the careers of the Beastie Boys, L.L. Cool J, Run DMC and Public Enemy?

3. Wallace Amos, Jr. is the African American founder of what company and product?

Answers From Yesterday

1. A.C. Green
2. Tyra Banks
3. Booker T. Washington

BLACK FACTS

Ellen and William Craft

HISTORY

Cross Dressing • Ellen and William Craft escaped from slavery with clever disguises and quick thinking. In 1847, the husband and wife traveled from Georgia posing as master and slave. Ellen, who was light skinned enough to be mistaken for white, dressed as a young man in a black suit, cloak and high-heeled boots. She covered her beardless face by wrapping it with cloth, claiming to have a severe toothache.

Unable to read or write, Ellen avoided signing hotel registers by keeping her arm in a sling as if it was broken. She also pretended to be deaf so she wouldn't have to speak in her natural voice. William did all the talking when his "master" had a need. All these strategies worked and they were treated as gentleman and slave, staying in first class hotels in Charleston and Richmond.

They almost got caught in Baltimore when officials insisted that a bond be posted for William, required "for all Negroes traveling north." But William protested that his master was in delicate health, and must reach expert medical care in Philadelphia to save his life. William's devotion to his young master touched the officials' hearts and they made it to Philadelphia.

Later, they traveled to Boston and once there, they openly told their story. The news of their successful masquerade was reported all over the country. After the Civil War, they traveled back to Georgia and bought a plantation near their old home.

The Other King • On March 3, 1991, 25 year old **Rodney King** led police on a high speed chase through Los Angeles. King was on probation for a robbery conviction. Once it was over, King was pulled out of the car and severely beaten with nightsticks and shocked with electric prods. What made this beating exceptional was that it was captured on video tape by a bystander. Many who saw the tape were horrified by it, including President George H.W. Bush.

But a predominately white jury in Sylmar, CA found the officers not guilty. The verdict set off one of the worse riots in American history. The federal government indicted the officers on charges of violating King's civil rights. After another long trial, three of the four officers were found guilty and sentenced to prison. Rodney King was awarded 3.8 million in damages from the city in a settlement.

Do You Know???

1. What African American musician is credited for single handedly redefining the sound of the electric guitar, and setting the standard for musicians ever since?

2. Who was the African American heavyweight boxing champion who held the title for over 11 years, the longest period in the history of the sport?

3. What was the surname **Malcolm X** refused to use, since it did not reflect his ancestral identity?

Answers From Yesterday

1. James Earl Ray in Memphis, TN
2. Russell Simmons
3. The Famous Amos Cookie Company

February 24, 2012

BLACK FACTS

HISTORY

Roots of Rap • The term "rap" is from the word *rapport*, which means understanding between friends. Rap music is storytelling in loose rhymes by one or more speakers over a musical selection, often borrowed or "sampled" from another artist. Rapping has roots that go back to Africa and the Caribbean, especially Jamaica. As a musical form, rap can be traced back to scat singing in jazz groups in the 1950's.

It wasn't until the 1970's however, that a core group of DJ's (or MC's), emerged in New York. The term "hip-hop" was coined to describe the ability to jump back and forth between selections on various records, to create new songs out of them. At the same time, black street rappers began reciting poetic stories about love, violence and life's struggles, over music played on huge cassette players called "ghetto blasters."

Then in 1979, this new art form burst on the nation when the first rap hit, "Rapper's Delight," was released by the Sugar Hill Gang. Over time, rap music has been controversial because of its connection with street culture and its reflection of black youth's anger and frustration with American society. Rap has also been condemned for some artists' use of profane language and offensive lyrics.

At the same time however, Rap music has had a tremendous influence on many aspects of mainstream American culture, from dress, to movies, television, and even our everyday language.

Montgomery, AL, 1955 – **Mrs. Rosa Parks** took a seat in the front of a Cleveland Avenue bus and was arrested when she refused to surrender it to a white man. Four days later, Dr. Martin L. King Jr. urged the city's black community to boycott the buses. The Montgomery Bus Boycott was the start of the nonviolent movement which led to the Civil Rights Act of 1960.

FIRSTS

Dr. Solomon Fuller was a pioneer in the field of treating mental illness. He was born in Liberia and moved to the U.S. where he became a medical doctor in 1897. He was one of the first to do research on schizophrenia and Alzheimer's disease. Many of his theories on mental disorders have proven to be accurate. Dr. Fuller was one of the first to practice psychotherapy: treatment through counseling and discussion to help patients analyze their own behavior and feelings.

Handicap ▪ **Charlie Sifford** was the first African American golf champion. He won the Los Angeles Open in 1969, making him the first Black player to win a  major golf event in the U.S. He also won the Puerto Rico Open in 1964, the Hartford open in 1967, the PGA Senior's Open in 1975 and in 1980. Over his long career, he earned close to $600,000.

Dinner Guest- ▪ On October 16, 1901, President Theodore Roosevelt invited **Booker T. Washington** to stay for dinner after a meeting Washington had with the president. He accepted and so became the first African American to dine with a U.S. president in the White House.

TRUE OR FALSE???

1. Tiger Woods was the first Black golfer to play in the Masters Tournament

2. Kwanzaa was invented by an African College professor in the 1960's.

3. The Million Man March in 1995 drew almost one and one-half million participants.

Answers From Yesterday

1. Jimi Hendrix
2. Joe Louis
3. Malcolm X was born Malcolm Little

February 27, 2012

BLACK FACTS

HISTORY

BLACK REPUBLICANS • The Republican Party began as a political group working to fight against slavery and other issues. Abraham Lincoln was their candidate for president in 1862. Black voters were naturally drawn to the party and were loyal members for about 75 years. All of the Black congressmen elected after the Civil War were Republican. However, during the 1930's, Republican President Herbert Hoover was perceived as not caring about those hit hard by the Great Depression.

Democrat Franklin Roosevelt struck a chord with African Americans. It was Roosevelt who began many federal government programs which provide help for the poor, the elderly, etc. Steadily, Blacks left the Republican Party and became Democrats. Most have remained loyal, some believe too loyal, to the Democratic Party ever since.

INVISIBLE EMPIRE In 1865, a group of six ex-confederate soldiers began a fraternity in Pulaski, TN, which they called the Ku Klux Klan. The name came from the word "kykios" which in Greek means "circle" and from the word "clan" which in Scottish means "family." The original purpose of the group was not focused. They wanted to do something to maintain white's superior place in southern society. They rode around wearing sheets to make blacks believe ghosts of dead rebel soldiers were haunting the hills, but did not seriously harm anyone. In 1867, however, the Reconstruction Act gave black people full civil rights, including the right to vote. At a meeting in Nashville, the KKK re-created itself into an organization with a clear agenda: do what was necessary to keep blacks in their place. The first Grand Wizard was Nathan Forrest, one of the original six founders. But Forrest had no idea just how far the Klan's ranks were willing to go. Shocked by the sheer terrorism of the Klan, he directed the organization to be disbanded in 1869, but he was ignored. The Ku Klux Klan had grown into a monster the founders could no longer control.

FIRSTS

Andre Watts was the first African American concert pianist to achieve international stardom. By the age of nine, he was already performing with the Philadelphia Orchestra. In 1962, music legend Leonard Bernstein of the New York Philharmonic chose Watts as a last-minute replacement for an ailing pianist for a concert. At the end of his performance, the 16-year old Watts got a standing ovation not only from the audience, but from the orchestra as well. Today, Andre Watts is in huge demand as he performs with great orchestras around the world. His recordings of classical music are also considered to be some of the best.

DO YOU KNOW???

1. What is the name of the character made so popular by black puppeteer **Kevin Clash**?

2. What was the first African American organized religious denomination in the US?

3. What is the most common last name of blacks in the U.S.?

Answers From Friday

1. FALSE - The 1st was **Lee Elder** in 1975.

2. TRUE - **Maulama Karenga** created it in 1966.

3. FALSE - The march drew around 870,000.

SKC Publications, 2012

The Nicholas Brothers

February 28, 2012

BLACK FACTS

HISTORY

The most beloved dance team in entertainment history is **Fayard** and **Harold Nicholas**, known as the Nicholas Brothers. They grew up in Philadelphia, raised by musician parents who played in their own band. Neither brother had any formal dance training. The brothers astonished their audiences with their acrobatic spins, twists, flips, and tap dancing to jazz tempos. One of their signature routines was to dance down a huge staircase, leapfrogging over each other and landing in a complete split each time.

The Nicholas Brothers starred in shows all over the world. They appeared in movies, television shows, nightclubs, and theaters; and also performed for American troops overseas. The brothers taught master classes in tap dance at Harvard University. Their known students include Debbie Allen, Janet Jackson, and Michael Jackson.

Dance great Gregory Hines once stated that if their biography was ever filmed, their dance numbers would have to be computer generated, because no one could ever recreate them. Ballet icon Mikhail Baryshnikov declared that they were the most amazing dancers he had ever seen in his life.

Soul Train was the first black - oriented music variety show ever offered on American television. The series was created by **Don Cornelius**, who was its first host and the executive producer. The show's format included guest musical performers and hosts. Set in a dance club environment, the show also featured young women and men, dressed in the fashion of the day, who danced to the most popular songs on the R&B, Soul, and Rap charts. It aired from October 1971 to March 2006, making it the longest first-run syndicated program in television history.

SKC Publications, 2012 ©

19

FIRSTS

Colonel Robert Lawrence, Jr. was the first black astronaut for NASA. He was highly decorated Air Force pilot with a PhD in Chemistry. His outstanding career came to an end at age 32, when his F-104D Starfighter Jet crashed on a runway in 1967.

Female Astronaut ▪In 1992, **Dr. Mae C. Jemison** became the first African American woman in space. Aboard the U.S. space shuttle *Endeavor,* she studied the behavior of living organisms in space. Dr. Jemison is both a physician and a chemical engineer.

Barack Hussein Obama II is the 44th president of the United States and the first African-American president in American history. His father, from Kenya, and his mother, from Kansas, met at the University of Hawaii. After his parents divorced, Obama stayed with his mother and was raised in Indonesia and Hawaii. He graduated from Columbia University in 1983 and from Harvard Law School in 1991. Obama married the former Michelle Robinson in 1992. They have two daughters, Malia and Sasha. Obama taught constitutional law for 12 years at the University of Chicago. He was elected to the Illinois Senate in 1996, and then to the U.S. Senate in 2004. Barack Obama ran for president in 2008 and defeated Republican John McCain. He took office on January 20, 2009. Obama was also awarded the Nobel Peace Prize in 2009.

Do You Know???

1. What is the name of the college in Florida that was founded by a black school teacher?

2. True or False? Martin L. King was nearly killed in Harlem by a black woman who stabbed him in the chest with a letter opener.

3. What noted African American said the following: "Everybody can be great, because everybody can serve."?

Answers tomorrow…

Answers From Yesterday
1. Elmo of *Sesame Street*.
2. African Methodist Episcopal (AME) Church
3. The most common name is *Johnson*, followed by *Williams*, then *Jones*.

Mr. Frederick Douglass

BLACK FACTS

HISTORY

MR. DOUGLASS ▪ Frederick Douglass was the most prominent black leader of the 19th century. He was born a slave on February 14, 1817. Despite the law against it, his mistress taught him to read and write. When his master died, he was sold and then sent out to do field work. He was whipped often for his resistance to slavery. In 1838, Douglass escaped by disguising himself as a sailor, and was able to reach New York.

In 1845, he bravely published his autobiography which told of his life as a slave and exposed him to the danger of re-enslavement. He spent two years traveling and speaking in Europe, which allowed him to raise enough money to buy his freedom. Douglass returned to the U.S. just before the Civil War. After meeting President Abraham Lincoln, he helped form the Massachusetts 54th and 55th regiments, the first black regiments of the war.

Douglass was very involved with the struggle for civil rights. His tireless work on behalf of African Americans, and his personal dignity as he walked among presidents and kings, made him an unforgettable hero in history.

BLACK NATIONALISM ▪
Marcus Garvey is the most well-known black nationalist in US history. He was born in Jamaica in 1887 and spent his early adulthood working for social reform. In his travels, Garvey found blacks living in similar poor conditions in many parts of the world. He became convinced that the best hope for black people's future was to build separate societies from whites. In 1914, Garvey founded the Universal Negro Improvement Association. At its peak, the UNIA had about two million members. Garvey's lack of management skills lead to the UNIA's decline. Mail fraud charges lead to Garvey's imprisonment for a five year term. Later he was deported to Jamaica, where he died in 1940.

EBONICS, a blend of the words *ebony* and *phonics*, simply means "black speech." A group of black scholars who disliked the negative connotations of the phrase, "Nonstandard Negro English" created this term in 1973, but it never caught on with the general public. That all changed in 1996, when the Oakland, CA School Board declared Ebonics to be the "primary language" of African American students. Black writers have often used Ebonics in their work, and many have praised it as culturally authentic.

However, many other people, black and white, regard such speech as a sign of limited education or sophistication; as a legacy of slavery; or as a hindrance to socioeconomic success. One thing is sure: this distinctive way of speaking is thoroughly intertwined with African American history and culture, and it will probably continue to be heard for many years to come.

FIRSTS

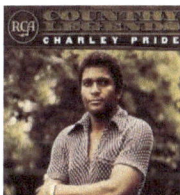

Charlie Pride was the first black superstar of country Music. He is a three-time Grammy Award winner and has recorded over 30 albums. He was the first African American to become a member of the Grand Ole Opry. In 1970, he was named Country Music Entertainer of the Year.

Answers From Yesterday

1. Bethune-Cookman College, in Daytona Beach, was founded by Mary McCleod Bethune.

2. True. Izola Curry stabbed him close to the heart in 1958. She was later committed to a mental institution.

3. Dr. Martin Luther King, Jr.

There is so much more… African Americans should be proud of the contributions they have made to the US and the world. Despite great obstacles, much has been achieved and even more is possible in the future!

Sources

Aquifer American Social History Online Project. *American History Online.* (2007-2011). http://www.americanhistoryonline.org.

Ciment, James. *Atlas of African-American History.* New York: Checkmark, 2001.

Harvey, Edmund H., Jr. *Our Glorious Century.* Pleasantville, NY: Reader's Digest, 1994.

Stewart, Jeffrey C. *1001 Things Everyone Should Know About African American History.* New York: Random House, 1996.

United States Library of Congress. *The Library of Congress: American Memory.* African American History Collections . February, 2001. http://www.loc.gov/index.html.

NAME INDEX